The BABY is COMING

Andre' Renee Harris

Illustrated by
Felicia Whaley

The Baby is Coming

The Baby is coming © 2017 Andre' Renee Harris
All rights Reserved.

Published by Andre Renee Writes Publishing Co, LLC
No part of this publication may be reproduced, or stored in a retrieval system, or transmitted by any form or by any means (electronic, mechanical, photocopying, recording, or otherwise), without written permission from the author. Without permission from the author/publisher, reproduction is considered illegal and punishable by law. Your support of the author's intellectual rights, are appreciated.

ISBN 13: 978-1976122682
ISBN 10: 1976122686

Printed in the U.S.A.

www.andrereneewrites.com

EAST CHICAGO PUBLIC LIBRARY
EAST CHICAGO, INDIANA

The Baby is Coming

Andre' Renee Harris

Illustrated by

Felicia Whaley

Preface

This book provides an opportunity for families to spend time together while enjoying exceptional literature.

My Mommy's belly is getting so big! I have a little brother or sister in there, Niyah thought to herself as she filled with joy.

Joseph, Niyah's dad, described how the new baby lives in mommy's belly.

"Niyah, for nine months your little brother or sister has been growing in mommy's belly," Dad explained.

"Daddy," Niyah asked, "what does the baby eat?"

Daddy answered, "Whatever Mommy eats, and we have to make sure she eats healthy, then the baby will grow to be big and strong."

Niyah insisted, "Mommy I'm going to help you eat right, I will eat all the candy so you can be healthy!"
Niyah's parents both laugh.

At school, Niyah told all of her friends that she is going to have a new baby brother or sister coming very soon from her mother's belly. One of her friends shouted,

"We have a dog, she had puppies in her belly.

When I came home from school there were seven baby puppies waiting there to greet me."

A confused Niyah asked, "Daddy, is Mommy going to have seven babies like my friend's dog at school did?" Joseph exclaimed, "SEVEN!"

"Yes Daddy," Niyah added, "when my friend came home from school, there were seven baby puppies that came from the mommy dog's belly."

Joseph laughed and explained that pets and Mommy's are made differently.

"Mommy will not have seven puppies or babies," Dad chuckled.

Niyah giggled, "Daddy, I wish I could have a brother and a puppy too!"

The next day, while Niyah was at school, her mom went into labor and had to be taken to the hospital. Niyah's Dad came to the school, to take her to the hospital. As they left the school together Dad exclaimed,
    "The BABY is coming!"
On the way to the hospital, Niyah asked, "Is the baby here yet?"
Joseph replied, "Almost baby, almost."

As soon as they arrived at the hospital, the doctor rushed Joseph into the delivery room,
to watch the baby make its first appearance.

Joseph and Jada cried with joy, "The baby is here and it's a BOY!"

Mom and Dad both agreed that Niyah should name her new baby brother.

Niyah entered the room, and held her brother for the first time. She smiled and said, "My brother's name is Joseph, like Daddy's, and like Daddy, I will love him forever."

Mom and Dad were both beaming with happiness.

Niyah jokingly added, "Now that I have a baby brother,

where's my puppy?!"

Everyone in the room laughed.

Andre' Renee Harris

As a writer of children's books, I believe teaching children early to get along with one another is paramount to life, peace and growth. In my series of children's books, the goal is to do just that. Our future generation is the most important focus of my life. My purpose is to channel all the positive energy I can into my writing. I strongly believe that children are never too young to be exposed to a variety of cultures. Humanity will depend on us. As caretakers of young minds, we must do our due diligence when educating them. We are tasked with cultivating a new generation, so that they will be afforded social provisions, to take humanity to greater heights.

Education is the fertile ground needed to plant our children. Nurturing children through literature brings wonder and amazement to their lives. As they grow, it becomes more apparent how vital it is to forge strong alliances, among all people, across all nations and beliefs.

The Baby is Coming

The Harris family is expecting a new bundle of joy. Will Niyah be getting a sister or brother? Maybe even a puppy.

Check out These other titles to complete your trilogy:

Made in the USA
Columbia, SC
13 September 2017